How have things changed?

At School

James Nixon

W

FRANKLIN WATTS
LONDON • SYDNEY

This edition published in 2013 by
Franklin Watts
338 Euston Road
London NW1 3BH

Franklin Watts Australia
Level 17/207 Kent Street
Sydney NSW 2000

ISBN: 978 1 4451 1853 6

Dewey classification number: 371

A CIP catalogue record for this book is available
from the British Library.

Planning and production by Discovery Books Limited
Editor: James Nixon
Designer: Rob Norridge

Photographs: p6 Nottingham City Council and www.picturethepast.org.uk, p7 Bobby Humphrey, p8
Mary Evans Picture Library, p9 Bobby Humphrey, p10 Haywood Magee/Getty Images, p11 Bobby
Humphrey, p12 Nottingham City Council and www.picturethepast.org.uk, p13 (top) Bobby
Humphrey, p13 (bottom) Chris Fairclough, p14 (top) Milton Keynes Museum, p14 (bottom) Getty
Images, p15 (top) istockphoto.com, p15 (middle, bottom) Bobby Humphrey, p16 (top) Derek
Berwin/Getty Images, p16 (middle) Nancy Honeycutt/istockphoto.com, p16 (bottom) Bobby
Humphrey, p17 (top) Bobby Humphrey, p17 (middle) Chris Fairclough, p17 (bottom) Bobby
Humphrey, p18 Mary Evans Picture Library, p19 Bobby Humphrey, p20 Courtesy of Nottinghamshire
County Council and www.picturethepast.org.uk, p21 Bobby Humphrey, p22 Getty Images, p23 Bobby
Humphrey, p24 Getty Images, p25 Bobby Humphrey, p26 (top) H. Allen/Getty Images, p26 (bottom)
Henry Grant/Mary Evans Picture Library, p27 Bobby Humphrey.

Cover photos: (top) Mary Evans Picture Library, (bottom) Bobby Humphrey.

Printed in China

Franklin Watts is a division of Hachette Children's Books,
an Hachette UK company.
www.hachette.co.uk

Contents

How have schools changed?

Where do you go to school? What is your school like? When was your school built? Is it an old school or a new school?

1910

Schools have changed a lot in the last hundred years. Look at Bulwell Primary School in 1910. Most children then only went to school until the age of 12. Now children have to go to school until they are 16.

Today, some schools like Bulwell Primary still use the same building that they did a hundred years ago. Look how the building has changed. The bell tower and some of the chimneys have gone.

Now

Why did schools in the past need chimneys?

Then and now

How do Victorian school buildings look different from modern schools?

Now

Since the 1960s many schools have been replaced with more modern buildings like this one.

7

The classroom

Classrooms looked very different around a hundred years ago. Look at this classroom from 1905. The few pictures hanging on the walls were not made by the children. The windows were high up so children could not look out of them.

1905

Why are there only boys in this picture?

Then and now

Children sat in rows at wooden desks. Everybody faced towards the front.

How are the desks different from the ones on the next page?

Today's classrooms are usually much brighter. The pupils decorate the room with their own pictures and displays.

How does your classroom compare with the rooms in the pictures?

Now

These children are sitting around tables in groups. Most classrooms in primary schools have a carpet area where the whole class can sit down together.

Then and now

Which classroom do you think would be a better place to learn? Why?

9

Lessons

In the past, classes were often told to **chant** or sing lists over and over again to help them learn facts by heart.

Learning by heart

In history lessons pupils had to list the English Kings and Queens in order with no mistakes. In geography lessons you may have had to sing the name of every railway station between London and Holyhead in Wales.

1952

It was also common in the past for pupils to spend hours in silence copying work from the blackboard or their textbooks.

Today's lessons can be very different. In this maths lesson pupils have to work out sums when they catch the ball.

Instead of sitting in silence at their desks, children often work in groups. The teachers move around the class to help.

Group activities in this modern lesson include maths games on the computer.

Then and now

Do you think lessons are more fun nowadays? Why?

Subjects

Lessons a hundred years ago were mainly reading, writing or **arithmetic**. These subjects were known as the 'three Rs'. As time went on more subjects were taught, such as **foreign languages**. Boys and girls were split up for some subjects.

1936

Boys would have woodwork lessons. Girls would do **needlework** or cookery.

What do you think the boys are making in this woodwork lesson?

Now

Look at this modern woodwork lesson. Now girls and boys do every subject together and are taught the same things.

Why do you think boys and girls were separated for some subjects in the 1930s?

Today, there are even more subjects to learn. Schools are able to teach more music and PE because they have much better equipment.

Why do you think schools have better equipment today?

Pens and paper

The equipment pupils used a hundred years ago was very basic. Young children practised their writing and

sums by scratching on slates. The scratches could be rubbed off so the slate could be used over and over again.

1937

Where do you think these children kept their ink?

Older children used **steel**-nibbed pens that had to be dipped in ink. The pen had to be dipped every few words or it would run dry. These pens were still used in some schools in the 1970s.

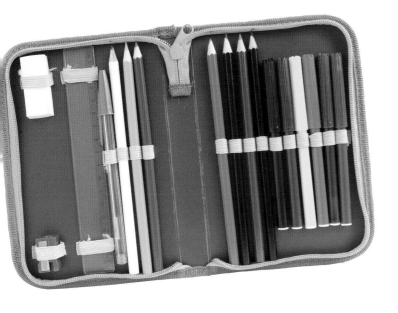

Today, children bring their own pencil case full of colourful pens, pencils, rulers and rubbers.

Children can now even type out work on a laptop computer in class. Many schools have an **IT suite** where the whole class can work on computers.

Find out for yourself

Make a list of all the equipment you use in school. What equipment on your list would not have been used in 1900?

Blackboard to whiteboard

For most lessons in the 1950s the classroom blackboard and textbooks were used. The chalk from the blackboard made the room dusty.

1956

1886

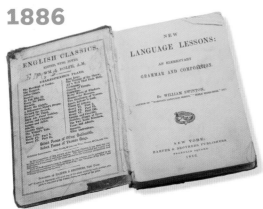

Textbooks in the past looked quite dull. In Victorian times the pages were black and white, and many had no pictures at all.

By the 1950s books were beginning to look more colourful. The texts were simpler and had more pictures.

1950

In modern classrooms whiteboards have replaced blackboards. **Interactive** games and activities can be played on the whiteboard.

Now

Despite the new technology, children will always learn from books as well.

Then and now

Look at these modern textbooks and compare them to the old ones. Which books do you think look more interesting?

Punishments and rewards

Teachers were very **strict** in the nineteenth century. Most children were terrified of their teachers. If you were naughty you were hit with a cane.

1820

Getting the cane

If you got something wrong you had to stand in the corner and wear the **dunce**'s hat (above, left). How would you feel if you had to wear the dunce's hat in front of all your friends?

Listed below are some reasons why pupils were punished with the cane:
- **Rudeness**
- **Bad temper**
- **Being late**
- **Throwing things in the classroom.**

Today, teachers are not allowed to hit children, but pupils still get told off.

Then and now

Do you think punishments were worse in the past? Why?

This girl and boy have been kept in at playtime because they have been badly behaved.

What do you think the boy in this picture is thinking?

Rewards

If children did well at school in the past they might have received an award. This certificate from 1903 was given to a child for their writing skills. What rewards do pupils get for good schoolwork in your school?

19

Uniform

Look at the uniforms in this photograph from 1910. Boys wore a jacket and **breeches**. The girls are wearing **pinafores**.

1910

Many children were from poor families at this time. This is why some of the clothes look ragged. All of the children are wearing **sturdy** boots. Why do you think this is?

Most schools still have uniforms today, but the style of clothes is more **casual.** In this modern class some children are wearing T-shirts and sweatshirts.

Then and now

Do you think the old or new uniform would be more comfortable to wear? Compare the teachers' clothes in each picture.

Now

Each school has its own uniform and **logo.** How many children in this picture are wearing the school logo on their clothes?

Travelling to school

In the 1920s a child might have had to walk a long distance to school.

1926

Imagine if the weather was cold and wet. The lanes could get very muddy. Children carried all their books in a leather **satchel**.

How would it feel to walk four or five kilometres to school like these children?

Today, if you live far away the school bus will pick you up.

What do you and your friends carry your schoolwork in today?

Your parents might take you to and from school in the car. You might even go on the train.

Find out for yourself

Do a survey of your classmates to see how they travel to school. Make a bar graph of your results. How do you think your results would compare to a class in 1920?

School meals

By the 1950s most schools were providing hot, cooked meals. There was often only one set meal and the food was sometimes horrible.

The teachers would not let you leave the table until your plate was empty.

1972

School dinners in the past were often not very healthy either. Can you see what these children from the 1970s are being served?

Schools today are trying to make their food a lot tastier, fresher and healthier.

Which foods being served in this picture do you think are healthy?

Now

Fatty foods such as burgers and chips are not on the menu most days, but there is a choice of meals to pick from.

Class Catering — HEART SMART — Menu — CLASS

Week 1

	MONDAY	TUESDAY	WEDNESDAY	THURSDAY	FRIDAY
	Sausages & Yorkshire Puds with Boiled Potatoes & Gravy	Beef Lasagne with Garlic Bread	Chicken Korma with Brown Rice	Roast Pork & Apple Sauce with Creamed & Roast Potatoes	Tuna Pasta Bake
	Roasted Vegetable Wraps with Crusty Bread	Pasta Provencal with Garlic Bread	Cauliflower & Broccoli Cheese with Herby Diced Potatoes	Leek & Mushroom Bake with Creamed & Roast Potatoes	Quorn Burger in a Bap with Chips
	Mixed Salad & Broccoli	Coleslaw & Sliced Carrots	Sweet corn & Carrots	Cauliflower & Swede	Peas & Baked Beans
	Treacle Sponge & Custard	Rhubarb Squares with Fresh Milk	Chocolate & Mandarin Muffin		

Week 2

	MONDAY	TUESDAY	WEDNESDAY	THURSDAY	FRIDAY
	Beef Bolognaise with Pasta Quills	Fish Cake with Parsley Potatoes	Roast Turkey with Creamed & Roast Potatoes	Apple & Cherry Crumble & Ice Cream	Neapolitan Sponge & Custard
	Quorn & Vegetable Lasagne with Garlic bread	Pasta with Tomato & Basil Sauce	Savoury Vegetable Slice with Creamed & Roast Potatoes	Beef & Vegetable Pie with New Potatoes	Chicken Fajitas
	Broccoli & Mixed Salad	Baked Beans & Green Beans	Carrots & Green Cabbage	Mediterranean Vegetable Risotto with Crusty Bread	Vegetable Stir Fry with Noodles
	Chocolate & Pear Delight	Jam & Coconut Sponge		Sweet corn & Peas / Cucumber Sticks & Grated Carrots / Oaty Apple Pie & Custard	Mixed Salad & Mini Corn on the Cob

Week 3

	MONDAY	TUESDAY	WEDNESDAY	THURSDAY	FRIDAY
	Oven Baked Burger with Sauté Potatoes	Roast Chicken & Stuffing with Creamed & Roast Potatoes	Fresh Fruit Salad & Shortbread Biscuits		Carrot Cake with Vanilla Icing
	Cheese & Red Onion Quiche	Cheesy Omelette with Creamed & Roast Potatoes	Turkey & Spinach Balti with Boiled Rice	Lamb Shepherds Pie with Boiled Potatoes	Salmon Tagliatelle
	Coleslaw & Tomato Salad & Baked Beans	Green Beans & Cauliflower	Cheese & Potato Bake with Crusty Bread	Vegetable Chilli with Boiled Rice	Cheese & Tomato Pizza with New Potatoes
	Sticky Toffee Pudding & Chocolate Sauce	Apple Flapjack with Fruit Juice Drink	Cucumber Riatta & Plum Tomatoes	Peas & Carrots	Green Salad & Sweet corn
			Apricot & Date Shortbread with Vanilla Sauce	Lemon Drizzle Cake	Iced Fruit Bun

Fresh cold drinking water will be available daily. A further selection of drinks to include—Water, Juice, Milk, Milkshakes & Smoothies will be available to purchase at middle schools only or as required.

A selection of breads & variety of salads will be available each day. A choice of Jacket Potatoes with a selection of fillings will be available daily as an alternative option where required.

Playtime

In the past, children brought in their own toys to play with at break times. In the 1930s playing with marbles was popular among boys.

1935

What are the boys carrying over their shoulders in this photo?

Games, such as hopscotch, follow-my-leader and clapping games, have always been popular because no equipment is needed.

By the 1970s schools were handing out toys such as balls, hoops and ropes at playtime.

1975

Schools now provide more equipment to play with at playtime. You might have a climbing frame and a football goal.

Look at the children in this modern school. Some are playing on stilts and pogo sticks.

Our Playground Rules

We play together and look after one another

We take care of our gardens and our equipment

We always tell if we feel frightened or sad

We stand still and stop talking when we hear the whistle

We walk sensibly to our lines

Traditional games are still popular as well. These pupils are playing a clapping game.

Then and now

What games do you play at break time? Would they have been played in the past?

Nowadays you may find a rule board in the playground. Does your school have playtime rules?

Glossary

Arithmetic Sums such as addition, subtraction, multiplication or division.

Breeches Short trousers fastened just below the knee.

Casual Describes clothes that are suitable for everyday wear.

Certificate A special piece of paper that gives proof of an achievement.

Chant To repeat a group of words over and over again.

Dunce A person who is slow at learning.

Foreign languages Languages, such as French or German, from other countries.

Interactive Describes a computer program that users can change and control.

IT Suite IT is an abbreviation for information technology. An IT suite is a classroom that has a computer at every desk.

Logo A small design.

Needlework The art of sewing.

Pinafores Full length sleeveless dresses worn over clothes to keep them clean.

Satchel A school bag that is carried on the shoulder by a long strap and closed by a flap.

Steel A hard, strong metal used on the nibs of pens that were dipped in ink.

Strict Describes teachers who are firm in making sure children behave properly and keep to the rules.

Sturdy Strong and solid.

Further information

Places to visit:

The Ragged School Museum, London (www.raggedschoolmuseum.org.uk)
This museum gives you a taste of school life for poor people in Victorian times.

Scotland Street School Museum, Glasgow (www.glasgowmuseums.com)
This museum presents a detailed history of education. It has three reconstructed classrooms from the Victorian era through to the 1960s. You can also listen to former pupils' memories of their schooldays.

Black Country Living Museum, Dudley (www.bclm.co.uk) Here you can see how a school would have looked a hundred years ago.

Milton Keynes Museum (www.mkmuseum.org.uk) Find out what Victorian lessons were like in the old schoolroom in this museum.

Visit your **local museum** or **local library** and see if you can find some history of your school.

Websites:

There are many websites where you can view historical photos of school life. Try the website of your **local council** and see if they have an image gallery. You may even find old photos of your own school.

www.maryevans.com
This site has lots of old images of schools on its database.

www.bbc.co.uk/schools/primaryhistory/victorian_britain/victorian_schools
This site has lots of photos and a video recreation of lessons in a Victorian school. It also has information, quizzes and activities on school life in the past.

Books to read:

A Victorian Childhood, Ruth Thomson, 2013 (Franklin Watts)
Schools (Life in the Past), Nicola Barber, 2012 (Wayland)
A Photographic View of Schools (Past in Pictures), Ales Woolf, 2013 (Wayland)
Around A School (A Walk), Sally Hewitt, 2012 (Franklin Watts)
School (Your Local Area), Ruth Thomson, 2010 (Wayland)

Index